Job Jungle

for
Career Awareness and Exploration

Stories and Illustrations
by

Laurie Barrows

Edited by

Francis Ferry

Acknowledgments

Grateful acknowledgment is given to Laurie Barrows for her special talents as a storyteller and artist.

Special thanks to Arthur Cutler, Robert Kauk, and Robert Robinett, authors of many career development materials.

To Janet Fiedler, teacher and coordinator of field testing the stories with second and third grade students.

To Toni Sanders, Janice Allen, and Linda Schwartz who helped in large and small ways with the production of ***Job Jungle***.

Job Jungle is dedicated to all children in primary grades. May their preparation to work be productive.

Dedicated to:
Lon, Brooke, David, Leanna, Logan, Brandon, and Chelsey, our grandchildren, who will join the work force in tomorrow's world -- Francis Ferry

CFKR Career Materials, Inc.
11860 Kemper Road, #7
Auburn, CA 95603

©1992 by CFKR Career Materials, Inc. All rights reserved. This book, or parts thereof, may not be reproduced in any form without written permission from the publisher.

ISBN 0-934783-48-9

Contents

Learning About Work 2

In The Classroom 4

Making A Movie 6

The Fruit Stand 8

Farmer Pig 10

Shopping 12

Surprise Party 14

Bugaboo 16

A Visit To The Doctor 18

On The Move 20

Summer Camp 22

Back To School 24

LEARNING ABOUT WORK

"What is **work**?" Owl, the **teacher**, asked the class. Some students had not thought about it before.

"Work is all the chores I have to do!" "Work is something you get paid for!" "Work is a job!" These were some answers the class gave Owl.

"All of your answers are good," said Owl. "Work is all the different **tasks** you do on a **job**. Work is something everyone needs to do. There are many different **types** of work. The type of work you do changes from job to job."

"Do you mean that there are different kinds of jobs?" Rabbit asked the **teacher**.

"Yes, Rabbit, there are many, many different jobs!" Owl replied.

"But why should I work?" wondered Bear aloud.

"Work is something of **value**, Bear," answered Owl.

"Do you want to feel **needed**? Do you want to feel **wanted**? Do you want to feel that what you do is **important**? Do you want to **earn** money?" Owl asked Bear.

"Yes I do," Bear answered, after thinking about it for a moment. "I want to **feel special**."

"Work helps us feel better about ourselves. A job gives us **self-respect**," Owl told the class.

"How is work different from a job?" asked Rabbit.

"All the different work you do makes up a job. A job may include many tasks," Owl answered.

"So everything we do at school is work. Our job is to go to school and to **learn**!" Rabbit exclaimed.

"Yes, Rabbit! Your job now is to go to school to learn. From your first day of school, you are getting special **training**. That **training** will help you choose the kind of work you will want to do as an adult," Owl explained.

Owl was happy that the class **learned** about work.

Bear, Rabbit, and all of their classmates felt very grown up.

They have a **special job** to do!

IN THE CLASSROOM

One day Bear and Rabbit's **teacher**, Owl, gave them a special homework assignment.

The assignment was to **team** up with a friend and do a report on an **occupation**.

The friends could choose the **occupation** on which to report.

"What should we find out about?" they wondered.

Bear thought about different **jobs**.

Rabbit liked the idea of **jobs** that **help** others.

They got some **ideas** from their **parents**.

They talked about their **likes** and **dislikes**.

Together, they decided to find out about different jobs for **helping** others.

Once they made their **decision**, they began to work.

Bear and Rabbit spoke with their **school counselor**, Fox, to get some ideas on helping jobs. Fox gave them some **information** and suggested they go to the library.

"Thank you," they said to Fox, and walked to the library.

At the library, Opossum, the **librarian**, helped Rabbit and Bear. Opossum told them how to look for books on jobs.

The two friends worked together to find some interesting **helping jobs**.

They took notes on **job requirements**.

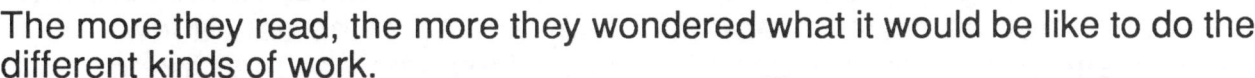

The more they read, the more they wondered what it would be like to do the different kinds of work.

They learned that sometimes they could train to work **on-the-job**, and that some jobs required a lot of **education**. Bear and Rabbit learned that **education** is important in preparing for a job.

A few days later, Rabbit and Bear were ready to report to their class. They told the other students that the **world of work** is interesting. Some of the jobs they talked about were a **barber**, a **flight attendant**, a **gardener**, and a **nurse**.

They told how their **teacher**, Owl, their **school counselor**, Fox, and the **librarian**, Opossum, all had jobs that helped others.

Bear and Rabbit **worked** hard on their report. They **learned** a lot about jobs.

They were happy to get a good grade for their hard **work**.

They were happy to help their friends **learn** something new!

6

MAKING A MOVIE

Bear and Rabbit were watching the TV news. Parrot, the **newscaster**, told a story about the new rose garden in the park.

The next story was about a new movie to be made in the park. The **producer** and **director** of the movie said that there were job openings to help make the movie.

Parrot announced that everyone interested in applying for a job would need to be at the park tomorrow by 8:00 AM sharp!

"It would be fun to make a movie!" exclaimed Bear. "I've always wondered how movies are made," said Rabbit.

Rabbit and Bear got up early the next morning. They dressed carefully and made sure they were **well groomed**. They arrived at the park a few minutes **early**. All their friends were there. They stood by their friend, Weasel, and visited a few moments.

Tiger was the **announcer**. Over a loud speaker Tiger said, "Attention, everyone! Quiet, please! I'd like to introduce Walrus, the **producer**, and Iguana, the **director**."

Everyone quieted down as Walrus spoke over the loudspeaker.

"I would like to thank you all for coming today," said Walrus.

Walrus then announced, "As the **producer**, it is my job to make sure that everything runs smoothly while making the movie. Iguana, the **director**, will tell everyone how the movie is to be made. Iguana will tell the **actors** how to act and the **camera operator** what to film, so the movie will be the best that it can be."

Walrus gave the loudspeaker back to Tiger. Tiger asked everyone to break into **groups** for the jobs that interested them.

Actors, **dancers**, and **musicians** were to go with Iguana to audition for a job.

Designers and **artists** were needed to help paint the movie sets. They met with Walrus.

Walrus chose an **art director** from the group to help the **producer** and **director** design the sets.

"I like to sing," said Bear, walking to the **musicians'** group.

"I like to act and pretend things, but not in front of others," said Rabbit, "but I can draw and I like to make things." Rabbit went with the **artists** and **designers**.

Weasel did not know where to go. "I'm not a **singer**, **dancer**, **actor**, or **artist**. But I am a good **writer**!" Weasel thought aloud. Weasel decided to write an article for the newspaper about movie making in the park.

Everyone found an interesting **job** to do to help make the movie in the park!

THE FRUIT STAND

One day Bear and Rabbit were walking in the country. They noticed some **work** being done in Farmer Pig's field.

Hippo, the **engineer**, was checking plans. Hippo was speaking with Lizard, the **architect**, and Alligator, the **contractor**, about the project.

Lizard made sure everyone agreed on how to do the **job** correctly and stay within the budget for the project.

The next day on their walk, Rabbit and Bear watched the tractors and dump trucks dig and move the dirt around.

Badger, the **excavation machine operator,** operated the back-hoe and dug trenches for a foundation.

Turtle, the **truck driver,** drove the cement truck. Turtle filled the trenches for the foundation with cement.

Ox, the **concrete mason**, made sure the cement was level.

A few days later, after the cement had dried, Rabbit and Bear heard power saws and the hammering of nails.

Chimpanzee, the **carpenter**, was busy framing the building.

Bear and Rabbit wondered what kind of building it would be.

The following day, Bear and Rabbit stopped to watch Toad, the **plumber**, install pipes for the water system.

Zebra, the **electrician**, began wiring for the electrical system.

All the while, Chimpanzee kept working on the framework of the structure.

The next week, Giraffe, the **roofer**, began to work on the roof.

Rabbit and Bear watched as Porcupine, the **glazier**, installed the windows.

Soon most of the electrical and plumbing work was finished.

Platypus, the **drywall installer**, began to install drywall on the inside walls of the building.

Bat, the **painter**, came to look at the new building. Bat and Farmer Pig discussed the color of the paint. Farmer Pig told Bat that the painting needed to be done by the following week.

Rabbit and Bear could see that the new building would be a fruit stand!

They congratulated Farmer Pig on the beautiful new building.

FARMER PIG

Bear and Rabbit went to visit **Farmer** Pig. **Farmer** Pig was busy planning a garden.

They went with **Farmer** Pig to the nursery to buy plants for the garden.

At the nursery, **Farmer** Pig spoke with Beaver, the **nursery manager**.
Farmer Pig asked Beaver, "Which type of plants would be best for my garden?"

"You must keep in mind climate and the growing season when choosing plants," said Beaver.

Beaver and **Farmer** Pig talked about **Farmer** Pig's garden. This helped **Farmer** Pig choose the best kinds of plants.

Rabbit, Bear, and **Farmer** Pig waited for Mole, the **nursery worker**, to show them where to find the plants and seeds.

Mole was helping Rhino, the **gardener**, and Aardvark, the **groundskeeper**.

Rhino and Aardvark needed roses for the new flower garden they were planting in the park.

Aardvark also needed new grass seed to patch the park lawn.

"What can I help you with today?" Mole asked.

"I need green bean seeds and two tomato plants," said **Farmer** Pig.

"Right this way, please," said Mole. Mole led them to the tomato plants and helped them choose healthy plants.

Mole took them to the seed display. **Farmer** Pig chose the green bean seeds.

Bear and Rabbit helped **Farmer** Pig carry the plants and seeds to Squirrel, the **cashier**.

After paying for the plants, they put them in **Farmer** Pig's truck.

They drove back to the farm.

Farmer Pig, Rabbit, and Bear spent the rest of the afternoon planting green bean seeds and tomato plants.

It was hard work. **Farmer** Pig made lemonade. They drank lemonade in the shade of **Farmer** Pig's porch, and planned a surprise party for Rhino.

SHOPPING

Soon it will be Rhino's birthday! Rabbit and Bear wanted to buy a special birthday present for Rhino. They saved money from their movie making jobs.

Bear saw an advertisement in the newspaper for a sale on hats. A new hat would be the perfect gift for Rhino!

Bear and Rabbit walked to the store. They went to the hat department. Emu, the **sales clerk**, helped them choose a hat. They could not find a Hawaiian print hat like the one in the ad that would fit Rhino.

Emu called Monkey, the **stock clerk**, to see if there might be another hat in inventory. There were no more Hawaiian hats, but there were sets of Hawaiian hats with matching socks. These were not on sale, and they cost more than Bear and Rabbit had to spend.

"Gee," sighed Rabbit, "I really thought the Hawaiian hat would be perfect for Rhino."

"I know," Bear replied. "We came all this way just for that hat! What will we do?"

Emu heard them talking and felt badly for them. "Wait just a minute," said Emu the **sales clerk**. "Maybe I can still help you."

Emu called Leopard, the **store manager**. Emu explained the situation to Leopard. Leopard said it was all right for Emu to sell the Hawaiian hat with matching socks for the same price as the Hawaiian hats that were on sale.

This made Rabbit and Bear very happy. They paid Emu for the hat and socks. Emu gave them their change. Emu put the hat and socks in a bag.

Rabbit and Bear took their purchase home. They wrapped it in bright paper.

They would take the present to Rhino's surprise party.

Wouldn't Rhino look grand in a Hawaiian hat with matching socks?

SURPRISE PARTY

It was Rhino's birthday!

Bear and Rabbit took Rhino out for lunch. Rhino did not know about the surprise party they had planned.

The three friends went to the restaurant.

Ostrich, the **host**, showed them to their table.

When they were seated, Rhino's friends came out of hiding and yelled, "SURPRISE!"

Wolf, the **police officer**, Elephant, the **firefighter**,
Sloth, the **dry cleaner**, Weasel, the **writer**,
and Hedgehog, the **hairstylist**, were there.

Rhino was surprised.

Soon, Penguin, the **food server**, placed big plates of peanut butter and jelly sandwiches on the table.

Ostrich, the **host**, helped pour lemonade.

Moose, the **baker**, cut the special birthday cake that was made for Rhino.

Everyone ate and laughed. They had a good time.

Rabbit and Bear gave Rhino the Hawaiian hat and socks.

Farmer Pig gave Rhino a basket of tomatoes and green beans.

Weasel wrote Rhino a special birthday poem.

"Thank you for such a good birthday!" Rhino said to everyone. "The best part is being with all my friends!"

Rhino had a very special day.

BUGABOO

Bear and Rabbit were gardening in their backyard.

Bear dug a hole to plant petunias. When Bear picked up the plant, there was a huge bug on the flower.

"Rabbit! Come look at this!" Bear cried.

Rabbit rushed over to Bear. Neither of them had ever seen such a beautiful bug before. The bug's shell was bright pink, with purple spots.

"I don't know what kind of bug this is," Rabbit said to Bear. Bear didn't know either.

Bear went into the house to get their book about bugs. They looked in the book for the bug, but could not find it.

They called Orangutan, the **biologist**. Rabbit told Orangutan about the bug.

"Did you discover a new bug?" asked Orangutan.

The possible discovery of a new bug excited everyone.

Orangutan ran all the way to Bear and Rabbit's house.

Orangutan called Buffalo, an **ecologist**, to come over to see the bug.

The **ecologist** came to see the bug.

The **biologist** tried to identify the new bug, while the **ecologist** wanted to know where the bug lived.

Orangutan, the **biologist**, could not identify the bug and decided to call Snake, an **entomologist**, for more help.

Buffalo, the **ecologist**, called Panda, a **botanist**, to come over to see the bug.

Soon, Bear and Rabbit's backyard was filled with all types of scientists.

Everyone was excited about the bug, but no one could identify it.

The bug, bored with all the goings on, flew away.

A VISIT TO THE DOCTOR

Bear and Rabbit were getting ready to go to summer camp, when Rabbit's ear started to ache.

Rabbit called Dr. Lion, the **pediatrician**, and spoke with Duck, the **receptionist**, to set up an appointment.

Rabbit went to Dr. Lion's office.

The **receptionist** took Rabbit's name and said, "Dr. Lion will see you in a few minutes."

Kangaroo, the **nurse**, lead Rabbit into an examination room.

The **nurse** took Rabbit's temperature, blood pressure, and listened to Rabbit's breathing.

The **nurse** wrote the information on Rabbit's chart for the doctor.

Dr. Lion came into the room and read **Nurse** Kangaroo's notes.

Dr. Lion asked Rabbit, "Which ear hurts?"

"My right ear," Rabbit responded.

"How long has it hurt?" asked Dr. Lion.

"My ear started hurting this morning," Rabbit answered.

Dr. Lion looked into Rabbit's ears with a special light.

"Hmm," said Dr. Lion, "you have an ear infection."

Dr. Lion wrote a prescription for medicine to make Rabbit's ear better.

"Be sure to take your medicine!" said Dr. Lion.

"I will," said Rabbit. "Thank you, Dr. Lion."

"Goodbye Rabbit. I hope you feel better soon," said Dr. Lion. Dr. Lion was glad to help Rabbit.

Rabbit went to the pharmacy to have the prescription filled.

Mouse, the **pharmacist**, read it.

Mouse followed Dr. Lion's directions carefully and prepared the medicine for Rabbit.

Rabbit paid for the medicine and took it home.

Rabbit followed Dr. Lion's instructions and soon felt better.

In a few days the infection was gone.

Now, Rabbit was up and hopping around, getting ready to go to summer camp.

ON THE MOVE

Vacation time!

Bear and Rabbit decided to travel by plane to summer camp.

They packed their bags and prepared to go by bus to the light rail station and then to the airport.

They carried their bags to the bus stop. The bus pulled up and Bear and Rabbit got on the bus. They paid the fare to Camel, the **bus driver**, and then found seats next to each other.

The bus carried them to the light rail station. Bear and Rabbit got off the bus.

They transferred to the light rail train to go to the airport.

Bear and Rabbit enjoyed the ride to the airport. They counted all the different types of cars, trucks, and other motor vehicles they saw on the road.

At the airport Bear and Rabbit got off the train with their bags.

"The terminal is so far away! My bag is heavy!" said Rabbit. "Let's take the shuttle bus to the terminal."

They walked to the shuttle stop and got on the next shuttle bus.

Bear and Rabbit rode the shuttle bus to the terminal. They saw lots of activity around the airport.

They watched a tank truck refuel an airplane. Riding past the control tower, they saw Albatross, the **air traffic controller**, who was making sure the planes in the air kept safe distances from each other.

The shuttle bus stopped at the terminal, and the two friends got off the bus. They thanked Cockatoo, the **shuttle bus driver**.

They carried their bags past some taxis and into the terminal.

Bear and Rabbit picked up their tickets at the ticket counter, and checked their bags to be loaded on the plane.

Bear and Rabbit walked to Gate C. They waited a few minutes before they could board their plane. They watched their bags being loaded on the plane. Then, they saw Eagle, the **pilot**, and Quail, the **flight attendant**, board the plane.

"Flight 123 is now boarding at Gate C!" a voice said over the loudspeaker.

Bear and Rabbit got in line to board the airplane. They showed Quail, the **flight attendant**, their tickets. Quail directed them to their seats. Bear and Rabbit sat down and buckled their safety belts. Soon, the plane took off.

They were excited to be on their way!

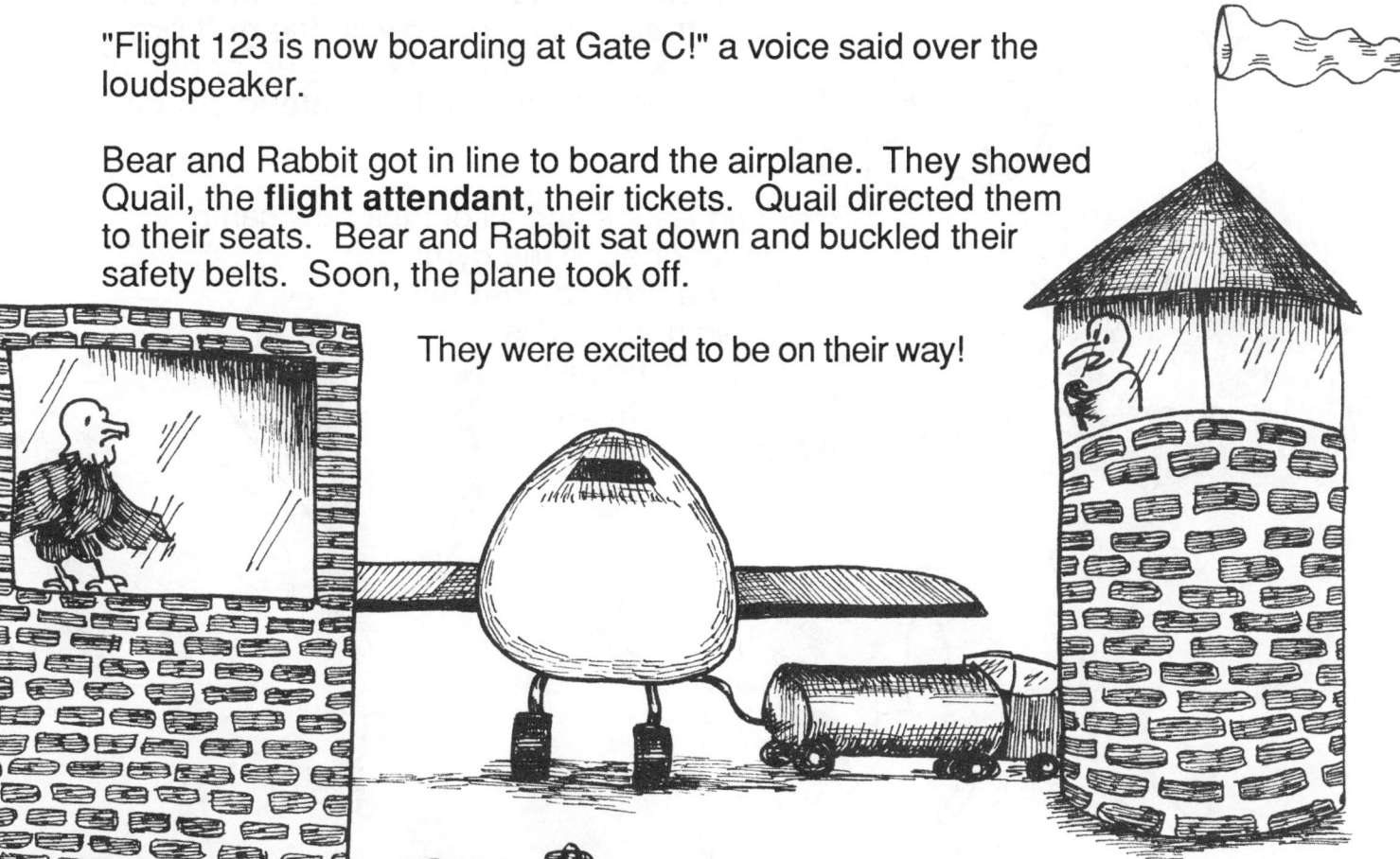

SUMMER CAMP

Bear and Rabbit said, "Goodbye, Eagle. We certainly enjoyed the airplane ride." When they got off the airplane, a bus was waiting to take them to Summer Camp.

At the camp they were welcomed by Llama, the **recreational leader.**

Llama said, "You need to report to Gorilla, the **fitness specialist**, for a fitness test. Gorilla will help you to decide on an exercise plan and help you to choose activities for the rest of the week."

"What activities will we be able to choose?" asked Rabbit.

"We have lots of activities, Rabbit," said Llama. "You may choose camping with the **camp director**, dancing with the **dance instructor**, golfing with the **golf pro**, hiking with the **park ranger**, or one of the other sports with the **athletic coach.**"

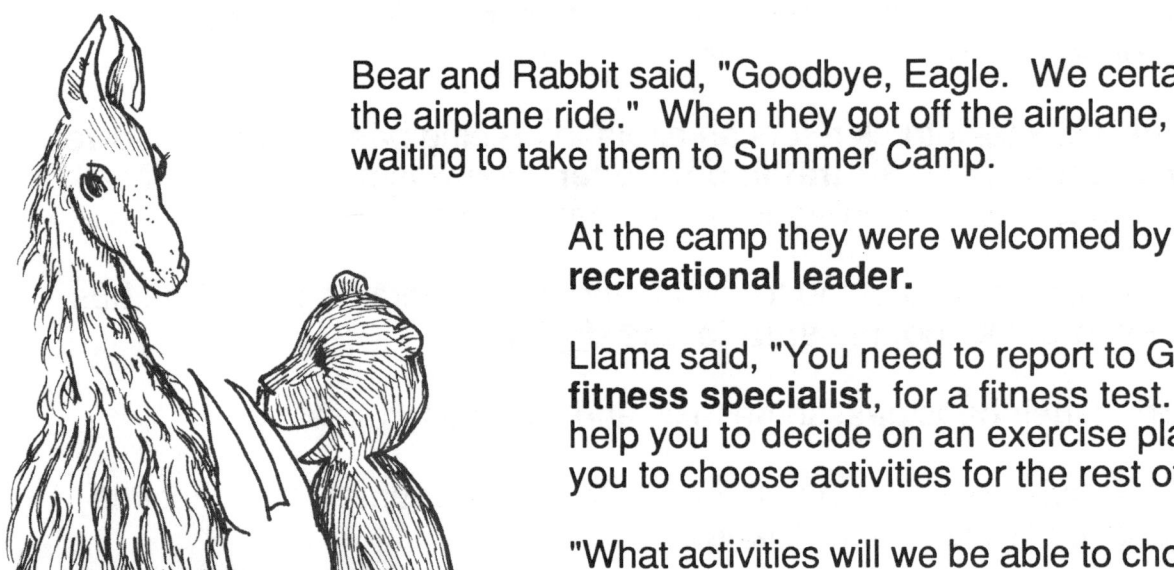

Bear and Rabbit and all of their new camp friends reported to the gym. Gorilla, the **fitness specialist**, evaluated their fitness. Then Gorilla helped them decide on an exercise plan.

Bear and Rabbit chose their activities for the week.

Rabbit went to an aerobic dance class. In the dance studio, Flamingo, the **dance instructor**, led the class in a dance exercise routine.

Bear decided to go swimming. At the pool, Octopus, the **locker room attendant**, gave Bear a clean towel. Seal, the **lifeguard**, guarded the pool to make sure everyone was safe.

Otter, the **swimming instructor**, was giving a swimming lesson in the shallow end of the pool.

In the afternoon, Bear and Rabbit played soccer. Raccoon, the **soccer coach**, instructed their team about teamwork. Roadrunner, the **referee**, made sure everyone played fairly and safely.

After dinner, Koala, the **activities director**, announced the evening programs.

Rabbit went to the arts and crafts room. Peacock, the **art instructor**, was giving painting lessons.

Bear joined a sing-along in the music room.

Bear and Rabbit and all their new friends had a wonderful time at summer camp! They were sorry that their vacation was over.

BACK TO SCHOOL

Bear and Rabbit returned home from summer camp. Vacation was over. "We had such a good time," Bear said to Rabbit.

"Yes we did," Rabbit replied. "Now we have to get ready for **school**."

The next day Bear, Rabbit and all their friends returned to **school**. Owl, the **teacher**, welcomed everyone back to **work**.

"Good morning students," Owl said. "I'm happy to see you and hope you will enjoy school this year. We have a lot to **learn**."

"What will we be **learning** this year?" Rabbit asked.

"We will be **learning** more about **mathematics** and **language**," answered Owl.

"These subjects will increase your **reasoning** ability, and will help you make good **decisions** and **solve problems**," Owl continued. "**Language** will also help you to be **understood** and to **understand** others."

"I want to learn about other things too!" exclaimed Bear.

"Yes, Bear," Owl replied, "we will learn more about **occupations**, **skills** and **work requirements** that are needed to be **successful** on the job."

"What are those **skills**?" asked Bear.

"Well, some of the **skills** are learned here at school," replied Owl. "When you come to school **on time**, and get your **work** done **on time**, you are **learning** an important **skill**."

Owl continued, "We will also learn other **skills**. We will learn to **work** skillfully with **things** and **ideas**, to **solve problems**, to **work independently**, to be **responsible**, and to **work** well with everyone."

"Wow!" exclaimed Rabbit. "We'll have to **work** hard this year!"

"Yes, we will **work** hard this year," Owl replied. "You will become more **aware** of your own **skills** and **interests** and be able to do better **work** in school."

Bear, Rabbit and all the students agreed.

Everyone had a **positive attitude** and looked forward to a happy school year.

Elementary Career Awareness and Career Exploration Materials Available from CFKR

Job Jungle

Job Jungle Activities

Career Discovery Encyclopedia (6 volumes)

Children's Dictionary of Occupations

Activities for Children's Dictionary of Occupations

E-WOW (Explore The World of Work)

JOB-O E

Looking at MySELF

Work Windows (Classroom Activities)

Self-Esteem Storybooks

Elementary Careers (Software)

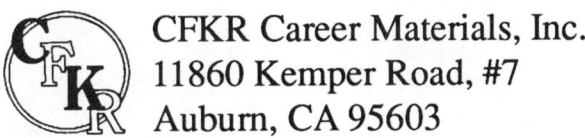

CFKR Career Materials, Inc.
11860 Kemper Road, #7
Auburn, CA 95603

Toll Free: 800-525-5626
FAX: (916) 889-0433